D1084624

My Aha Moments

Sharing the Journey

My Aha Moments

Sharing the Journey

May Rosanna Hsi

2019

Written in Honolulu, Hawaii
2018–2019

Book Design: Carolyn Vaughan (cvaughandesigns.com)

Printed in the USA.

❦ To My Parents ❦

Table of Contents

Foreword

I first saw Rosanna in 1960, when she was standing with two or three other students on the second floor at the head of a staircase in the Administration Building of Marymount College in Salina, Kansas. I was excited to be away from my hometown of 10,000 and attending college in the "huge" town of 40,000. To add to the stretch of a new life experience, here was a small woman—from Hong Kong—looking vulnerable and fragile, but somehow strong, alert, open. Someone was asking her if she spoke Mandarin or Cantonese. I wondered if I could get in on the conversation and somehow found my way in. The conversation has continued for nearly 60 years now.

When Rosanna came home with me at Thanksgiving, she was intrigued by the go-cart that some neighborhood boys were showing us. At the school playground across the street, she sat in it and listened as we explained how it worked. Someone must have pressed a button because suddenly the go-cart lurched forward and sped away. In panic, we dashed after the out-of-control cart. After a few harrowing moments, Rosanna pulled up alongside us and braked, her face flush with exhilaration. She was the one who had engineered the getaway—and had relished every minute of it.

I began to understand that this vulnerable, sensitive and seemingly fragile new Chinese friend was full of spunk and a zest for adventure. Always, she was stretching, seeking, evolving. But with all her engagement with the world, her priority has always been human relationships. Nothing drives or holds her more than deep connection with other human beings. That tenacious commitment emerges again and again in these 15 glimpses into her life. They are 15 gifts to all of us who have the privilege of knowing her.

Rosemary Jermann
May 2019

The best and most beautiful things in the world cannot be seen or even touched. They must be felt with the heart.

—Helen Keller

The Face of God

Una ola oloko ike aloha (Love gives life).

—Old Hawaiian prayer

It was Sunday again. The earthy odor of brewed herbs pervaded the house of my grandparents, tying my stomach into knots and filling me with dread. "It's time," my grandmother would say. "I know it burns, but the herbs will help to calm the inflammation." Then she cringed as she made her way through my cries of pain to wash my scalp.

My parents and I had moved from the village of Hing Ning to Canton, China, to live with my maternal grandparents when I was three. For over a year now, my head had been shaven and I had endured this weekly ritual. (The neighbors all called me the ugly duckling.)

Born prematurely, I had weighed only three pounds on my first day of life. My mother had carried me during the Japanese invasion of China, when there was little knowledge of prenatal care. She had often eaten her favorite rice gruel cooked with a tasty bottom-feeding scavenger fish, which today is considered toxic, especially for pregnant women. I have often wondered if that was the source of the scalp inflammation, digestion problems, and brain fog that plagued me as a child.

The latter would emerge when I began to attend Sacred Heart, a Chinese kindergarten in Hong Kong, at age six. My parents did not practice any religion, but my mother admired the discipline in Catholic schools. When the teachers there talked about God as love and goodness, it would be a new idea to me, as I had never heard about God at home.

At Sacred Heart, I quickly fell behind because of my inability to focus and finish assignments. I could not even make it through a simple story. One afternoon, my Aunt Pinky came to our house to help with my schoolwork. We began reading the children's book *Three Little Kittens*, but, unable to keep my eyes open, I fell asleep halfway through. Because I was often kept after school to catch up on assignments, other children laughed at me behind my back, made faces at me, and called me names. I felt like a misfit, and I was unhappy.

One morning, my homeroom teacher, Miss Pang, asked me to follow her into another room. *Had I done something wrong?* She sat me down and put a delicate chain of beads in my hand—a white translucent rosary. "This is for you," she said. "Pray the rosary." I stared down at the most beautiful gift I had ever received. She folded my hand in hers. "Mother Mary will help you in times of need," she said softly. I was moved to tears by this attention from the only person that ever noticed how miserable I was. Looking up at her kind and caring face, I wondered, *Is this what God looks like?*

The face of kindness comes in many forms. One morning in my tiny bedroom I was awakened by a beautiful voice. I opened my eyes to a loving face and sweet smile hovering over me. *Was it an angel?* "I'm Jun, your new nanny," she whispered. "I've come to take care of you." She reached out to me, and I sat up and hugged her. It was a common practice in Hong Kong to hire a nanny to care for children. My parents were often absent due to their busy work and social life, and the Chinese cultural norm was that parents did not raise their own children, but left that duty to their servants.

Every day Jun took me to school and picked me up. She was a petite woman with soft features and short, dark hair. She always wore a black top and black pants, the standard uniform for servants in those days. But what stood out in Jun was the love that exuded from her face and the smile she had for everyone. She was always waiting patiently for me at school while I stayed late to catch up on my studies. When others would say to her, "Oh, your young miss must not be too bright," she would fiercely defend me. I remember one day when I came out of school, crushed and weeping because of failing grades. Jun reached out her crooked, arthritic fingers and wrapped them around mine, and we walked home, hands intertwined. It was the greatest sense of unconditional love I had ever felt.

Eventually, we moved out of our first apartment. During my adolescence, when my parents were away in Japan due to my father's illness, Jun would come to the front gate with my white terrier Lolo (who would wet the floor with excitement) to welcome me home from school. My first question was always "Is Mom home?" And Jun's answer was always "No." I expected that answer, but felt let down each time. Jun's love helped to mitigate that feeling.

Our father had gone into the real estate business and was unexpectedly successful. In the sprawling mansion on top of Blue Pool Road, with its tiers of gardens, pavilions, and many rooms, I felt less lonely because my faithful dog and my nanny gave me a constant sense of love, security, and comfort. Walking the gardens with Lolo was a favorite pastime.

But even Jun and Lolo could not do away with the sense of forlornness and isolation that came when my parents were away in Japan for my father's medical treatment. When they returned, they were often occupied with the business, and I felt disconnected with everything, with everyone. I had nowhere to go, nothing to do. Once my mother summoned me and sternly asked if I was the one who had written "I am bored to death!" on my calendar. When I reflect now on what she was going through with my father's health, I realize how torn she must have been by what she read.

One afternoon, I heard shouting coming from the servant's quarters. When I went to investigate, I saw Jun sitting on her bed, crying, and her grown, red-faced son, yelling at her. When he saw me, he stormed out, slamming the door behind him.

"What happened?" I asked. "Why are you crying?" She wiped her eyes.

"My son is still very angry with me for not raising him myself," she said. Then she told me the story of how, as a widow, she had come to Hong Kong from Canton with her five children to escape the communists. "My husband smoked opium," she said, "and he died in an opium den fire." She went on to explain that, unable to provide for her children, she had had to send them out to different places so she could work to support them. "My daughters were much more understanding, but my son, never forgave me," she said sorrowfully. I was deeply stricken. For all the time she had taken wholehearted care of me, she had never hinted at her own suffering and heavy burden but had maintained a happy demeanor in our household.

When I went to study in the United States, Jun moved from Hong Kong to Vancouver to be closer to her daughters. Years later, when I lived in Hawaii, she came every year to visit me for a month. She remained as sweet and loving as she had been the morning when I had first laid eyes on her. She died in Canada in her 90s. When her daughter called to tell me of her death, I felt as if I had lost a mother. To this day I cherish the connection I still have with Jun's daughter.

The unconditional love and kindness of Miss Pang and Jun— each a hint of the face of God— left a formative imprint on me. Their loving and tender care had a nurturing effect that would make it possible to move beyond my own sense of inadequacy and to reach out to others in need.

Jun (my nanny) and I

The Voice of Suffering

Compassion is a social responsibility for human beings.

—Dalai Lama

I snuggled under the covers. Hong Kong winters are humid, and night had dropped on the city a bone-chilling cold that exacerbated the rheumatism wracking my eight-year-old body. We lived in a humble, ground floor apartment while my father worked very hard to make a living as a produce supplier for the British military. My small room, furnished with only a bed, was built onto the kitchen. To distract from the pain, I counted the pretty white mushrooms that grew abundantly on my ceiling and walls. I thought they were so cute but had no idea that what caused them to grow was the very thing that caused the painful rheumatism I had been enduring for some time. I knew it was eight o'clock, time to sleep, because the radio in the kitchen was playing the familiar, trumpet melody I heard every night. But due to the pain, sleep was not easy. When my nanny, Jun, came into the room, she saw my discomfort.

"Tell me where it hurts," she urged softly. "I'll massage you."

My mother had hired Jun to take care of me shortly after the time when, because of the chaos and turmoil in China, we had been part of the early mass exodus from Mainland China to Hong Kong. Regardless of qualifications or education, everyone fled in desperation, bringing almost nothing except their loved ones. Because so many Chinese refugees were in Hong Kong, hiring workers was very affordable and was common. That's how my beloved Jun came to our home.

With great tenderness, she massaged my painful joints. I relaxed and was about to drift off contentedly, when a man's heart-rending cry pierced the quiet. "Have mercy! Please have mercy on this blind beggar!" I bolted upright.

"What is that?" I gasped. Jun tried to calm me.

"It's a beggar I saw on the street today by the market. Now go to sleep." The man's pathetic cry persisted.

"Have pity on me! I am hungry and cold and blind." His cry knifed straight through to my heart. I had never heard anything like it. I knew it was bitterly cold, and I felt his anguish. Scanning the room, I spotted my piggy bank in a corner on the floor and exclaimed,

"Jun, please bring the money in my piggy bank!" She emptied the coins onto my bed, and we counted them. I told her to take all the money to the blind beggar.

"Are you sure?"

"Please," I said. "Give all the money to that poor man. Hurry, Jun!" So Jun went out into the cold to find the beggar who had wandered on to the next block. I listened intently as his pitiful cries faltered then fell silent. When Jun returned a few minutes later, she said that the man had thanked her again and again for the coins. "It's not from me," she had told him. "I have no money to give you. It is from my young miss."

The difference between the beggar and me was baffling. Here I was, cozy and secure in my warm bed, while he was blind, hungry, and cold. As I grew in years and experience, I would come to see such stark dualities of happiness and misery as two sides of the same coin of human life.

At that time, Maryknoll Convent School (run by the Maryknoll Sisters from New York, on the Kowloon Peninsula) was one of the best English language schools in Hong Kong. Accompanied by my nanny, I began to take the ferry and bus there each day and was thrown into the English-speaking world. For the entire first year I couldn't understand anything Sister Rosemary said as she talked a hundred miles an hour in her American English. Despite the language barrier, I was promoted and would continue to attend the school for the next decade of my life (1950–1960).

The teachers, almost all nuns, were missionaries, deeply devoted and committed to their students and their teaching. Many were educators, counselors, social workers, and medical professionals. The scope of their charitable work included the Canton Province of China, while in Hong Kong they opened schools and ministered to great numbers of the destitute migrants. In the late 1930s, thousands and thousands of Chinese families had fled to Hong Kong from Mainland China because of the Japanese invasion, the communist revolution, and the political upheaval and turmoil. Urban slums sprang up everywhere in Kowloon where the refugees

Rosanna at 12

were living in shelters made of tarps, tin, scraps of wood, and plastic bags. Once there was a terrible fire from a gasoline stove, and thousands of huts were burned to the ground in the settlement of Kowloon City. What pity I felt for all those families! The tragedy shook the whole of Hong Kong. The poorest of the poor suddenly became homeless. The Maryknoll nuns worked day and night to address their needs.

The impoverished communities needed help with medical treatment, counseling, education. Our teachers showed us photographs in class and always talked to us about what the Maryknoll sisters were doing. Their work instilled in us a great sense of social consciousness and purpose in alleviating the suffering of others. By their merciful actions, they showed us that we are indeed our brother's keeper—a sort of mantra I carry through my life. I believe that the caring was sparked that winter evening in my bedroom counting coins with my nanny. The ten years at Maryknoll, witnessing the unconditional service by the Maryknoll sisters—unconditional because it did not try to convert but simply sought to make God's love visible—helped the spark grow into a flame. Even today it is part of my spiritual practice to remember and send love to those who are suffering. The flame of caring has, in turn, sometimes kindled caring and action in those that I have touched.

Sister Mary Imelda, the Mother General of the Maryknoll sisters, was a special embodiment of the Maryknoll spirit of concern for the students. She knew my aunt, had helped me to get into the school, and would invite me to the convent to tea whenever she came to visit. A very gentle woman of virtue and spiritual profundity, she became my spiritual mentor. Before she was transferred back to the U.S., I asked her to make an entry in my autograph book. "My prayer for you," she wrote, "is that you will grow to be a woman who will live up to the motto of the school: *Sola Nobilitas Virtus* (Virtue alone ennobles)." In the years ahead, I would come to understand, that the greatest virtues are loving kindness and concern for others and that the greatest challenge would be putting them into practice in every way.

All That Glitters Is Not Gold

"What's all the commotion?" I gasped, astonished to see reporters and photographers crowding at the boarding gate.

"Don't you know? Lin Dai is on this flight." Could I really have hit such a jackpot? At the age of 15, on my first trip away from Hong Kong I was to be on a flight with the most renowned actress in Asia whose fresh beauty, talent, versatility, and charm I so much admired! What a story I would have for my mother's friend and her two daughters, Grace and May, who had invited me to Tokyo for the summer!

I settled into an economy-class seat, unable to contain the excitement of knowing that the actress was nearby in first-class. After we were airborne and the flight attendants were busy serving drinks, I could not repress the urge to go talk with her. Boldly I made my way to first class.

"Miss Lin," I asked, "may I sit with you?" Her momentary surprise was followed by a warm invitation to take the seat next to her. Under the spell of her eyes—deep pools of openness, not unlike those of Audrey Hepburn—I told her of my invitation to Tokyo and summer plans with friends. She listened with interest. I offered her a snack of the preserved ginger from my handbag. She commented on how lucky I was to have a mother so attentive as to provide me with a snack. Finally I broached what was really on my mind.

"Miss Lin, with your beauty, success, fame, and money, you must be the happiest person in the world." She looked at me intently now.

"*You're* the happy one"—her voice faltered ever so slightly—"with parents that love you, and even send you to Tokyo—for *fun.*" And she began to tell her own story of being an only daughter, of having an ambitious mother who goaded her incessantly to work harder to become rich, to bring prestige to her family. She felt used and unloved. Her eyes now seemed to be looking past me, and I could barely hear the next words: "I hope I can find love some day." "My young friend," she said, turning to me again, "appearance is deceptive. Beauty, success, fame, and money cannot bring happiness if there is no love. *There is nothing more valuable than to love and to be loved.*" Hearing the regret in her voice, I could think of nothing to say. When the captain announced the landing, I returned to my seat, moved—but also confused by trying to fit her words with what I had always believed. Having been brought up in Hong Kong, I was immersed in a materialistic culture where money and appearance counted heavily. Miss Lin's words made me look at what really mattered, and I couldn't stop thinking about it. When the plane arrived in Tokyo, Miss Lin was the first to disembark, was received with great pomp and ceremony, and was whisked away so quickly I had no chance for even a final glimpse of her.

Nearly ten years later, when I had finished my studies and returned to Hong Kong to teach, I met one of the most eligible bachelors in Hong Kong. Tall, dark, handsome, and from a banker family, he seemed to have everything and was much fawned over by many women. Remembering my encounter with Lin Dai helped me not to be seduced by the external trapping of his fame and fortune. What was even more important, we did not share similar values of the heart and spirit such as taking walks barefoot in the sand or being concerned about others. He was self-absorbed.

By that time, Lin Dai had taken her own life. It seems she never did find love or happiness. Her family had escaped from political upheaval in China to Hong Kong. As migrants they had undergone financial hardship. When her acting talent was discovered, she quickly rose to stardom and fame. Her mother pushed her to make more money for the family and later pressured her to marry for wealth and status. In a miserable marriage with a playboy, she was pulled more and more into the whole cycle of wealth, power, and fame and couldn't get out. But I could almost hear her words: "My young friend, nothing is more valuable than to love and be loved."

There was great astonishment when I turned down a proposal of marriage from the banker's son. *Why would she turn down a man who has everything?* When I heard this sort of reaction, I smiled with a deep gratitude welling up from my heart, and felt fortunate for my encounter with Lin Dai ten years ago. She had not found love, but her words had given me a solid sense of values and had set me on a path to happiness.

Agnes Arnsdorf

Words hold the power to change lives.
—Ancient Chinese saying

The heaviness as I walked into the chemistry class nearly stifled me. How would I make it through the Kansas summer heat and this incomprehensible class?

It did not help that the freshman year at Marymount College in Kansas had felt like a desert. It was not the people; they had an open, prairie gentleness. But after growing up on the island of Hong Kong, I was used to being surrounded by water and the verve and vitality of an Asian city. Without guidance from my parents or the school in the college application process, I had simply chosen the first four-year liberal arts school in the U.S. that accepted me. Shortly after arriving at a small town in the Midwest, I knew I was a fish out of water and had to make a change. But that change, a transfer to Holy Names University in Oakland, California, would occur only after this final class—if I could survive it. In the future, I would learn that destiny had brought me to Kansas for an important reason: to meet Agnes Arnsdorf— a woman of faith, wisdom, and love.

I immediately noticed Agnes in class because she was appreciably older than the rest of us—probably in her 40s. I saw her again at lunchtime in the cafeteria. A stout woman with short dark hair, she moved slowly, as if she were weighed down. Something drew me to her, and when she saw me, she smiled. We sat together for lunch, and that was the beginning of our friendship, which was the salvation of my summer school.

Agnes was easy to talk to. She was especially good to me when she realized I was a foreign student and that it was lonely for me in Kansas. She was friendly to the other students as well. When I told her that I was struggling because I hated chemistry and didn't see how I could possibly pass, she offered to help me. As we got to know each other, I think she came to see that I didn't have the mindset for chemistry. Bored and uninterested, I began to ask her questions that had nothing to do with science. "Agnes," I said, "let's talk about other things."

Agnes shared with me that she lived by herself and was suffering from poor health, including arthritis. She didn't go into much detail, though she clearly wasn't well. But she also loved going to school to learn new things and wanted to continue growing. "I never want to get rusty," she grinned. It impressed me that despite her health challenges, she came to class every day—to *chemistry* class—just to learn. She reminded me of a Chinese proverb that says there is no limit to learning.

One day during our lunch meeting, near the end of the summer session, I asked her to give me something to live by. "Agnes, what do you think is really important to know?" She took a moment before answering.

"For me, the most important thing is to be thoughtful of other people," she said quietly. "Most of the time"—she seemed to sigh a bit here—we think only of ourselves. And to be considerate of other people means being aware of them and respecting them."

Agnes's words may seem like common sense, but it was an "aha" moment for me. No one had ever said such a thing to me so explicitly. As a young woman, I had always assumed that everything revolved around me, that I was the center of everything. Agnes was giving me another way of seeing things, of seeing the world around me. Her words would pulse gently through the rest of my life, reminding me how to treat other people.

After the class that summer, I visited New York City, where I stayed in a Manhattan brownstone with a very nice Chinese middle-aged couple, friends of my mother. I don't remember that I did anything with them; I was there as a boarder, not as a houseguest. Young, independent, and a born traveler, I decided to also see Washington, D.C., for a few

26

days. But because of a serious delay of the train returning to New York, I arrived back at the brownstone early in the morning of the day I was to fly to California. With the prospect of just a few hours' sleep, I thought I could not possibly pack and catch the morning flight. Rescheduling and leaving the next day would be more convenient *for me*. Halfway through dialing TWA, I heard Agnes's voice: *whatever we do, we need always to be considerate of other people*. I started to consider my hosts. They had graciously let me live there for a week and were expecting me to leave today. An extension of my stay could be inconvenient *for them*. I hung up the phone and wildly flung my clothes into the suitcase. I thanked them and left as planned. Only later did I learn that my staying an extra day would have upset their plans to leave town.

The plane arrived in San Francisco that afternoon, and I settled in with my aunt and uncle in Oakland. The next day, near dinnertime, I happened to pick up a newspaper and was left breathless by headlines about the flight I would have taken had I decided to wait a day to leave New York: *TWA Flight 529 Crashes Just West of Midway Airport*. One of the first journalists on the scene noticed that there were no ambulances. That was because there were no survivors.

I called Agnes to tell her what had happened. She was grateful that I was safe. We kept in touch through letters for about seven years, although I never saw her after I left Kansas. Even in her letters, she remained the loving Agnes that I knew. She touched everyone she met. That was her mission, I believe. She was a living testimony of her Catholic faith, but she never tried to "teach" anyone; her influence came simply from who she was. I asked her many times to come visit me, but she could not. Her health kept deteriorating, and eventually she could no longer walk. When she did not answer my last letter, I sensed she had passed away. I feel privileged and blessed to have known Agnes. Living out of the wisdom she shared with me turned out to be the best thing I ever did for myself. Agnes would be happy and surprised to learn that my thoughtfulness has been noticed and appreciated by friends who, in turn, give it an important place in their lives—a testament to the far-reaching power of words.

Taking the Leap

Two roads diverged in a wood, and I—
I took the one less traveled by, and that has made all the difference.

—Robert Frost

This is a bad idea, I thought to myself as I boarded the plane from San Francisco to Hong Kong. *Why in the world was I going back home to live with my parents after five years of freedom?* It was 1965. I had finished my bachelor's degree from Holy Names University in Oakland, California, and my graduate diploma in education from the University of Durham in England. In Chinese culture, an unarticulated but deeply instilled obligation is that, after completion of studies abroad, we return home to spend some time with our parents. It is something we feel we owe to them. Because of the high cost of living in Hong Kong, those who have finished school live with their parents until marriage. Since four of my siblings had been sent away to boarding school in England, my parents had downsized, tearing down the mansion I grew up in to build a condominium, as one of their development projects. They then moved into a spacious apartment on the Peak with a spectacular view of the famous Hong Kong Harbor.

Upon my return, I was jolted by the changes. First, my sweet childhood memories of Hong Kong were shattered. The island was transforming from the slow and tranquil life I remembered into a fast-paced concrete jungle. Many low-rise and historical buildings had been razed to make room for commercial high-rise buildings and condominiums. Further, while growing up I had not been fully aware that

Hong Kong was a provincial, conservative English colony and was very class conscious. People were expected to act and dress a certain way, according to their station in life. Often one was judged by appearance, social status, and possessions (which represented wealth). My mother, who dressed in fashionable, tailor-made clothes, criticized me for my appearance. I loved to dress for comfort, but to her, I lacked taste.

When I left Hong Kong for school in the United States, I was a teenager who had been brought up to obey authoritative parents. When I returned to live with them, I was an adult who had been exposed to other values and had developed a mind of my own. I decided I wanted to teach. But my mother had other ideas.

"Why do you want to be a teacher? Wouldn't it be more prestigious to have your own school, to become a principal, and to open more schools?" I told her I just wanted to be a teacher. She was disappointed. I felt inadequate and that I could never live up to her expectations and standards. I was a butterfly trapped in a glass jar. The contrast of having experienced five years of freedom in the United States and England and now living with my parents was starting to feel confining. After the first year, I continued to question whether I should stay or leave. I decided to try it for another year to avoid making a rash decision.

During that second year, I started dating a banker's son, considered the most eligible bachelor in Hong Kong. Like me, he had also just returned to Hong Kong after studies in the United States. After we had dated for a few months, he proposed to me. I postponed answering him because I wasn't sure. On a crisp autumn day, as we were riding in his gold Rolls Royce, the long and winding road opened up to the turquoise waters of Repulse Bay, where I used to swim with my father. At that moment, I felt like flinging off my shoes and running in the sand. Impulsively, I turned to Roger and asked,

"Can we take a walk in our bare feet by the water?" He looked at me in disbelief.

"Take off my shoes and socks? How messy." In that moment, I knew we were not right for each other. It was the prelude to another "decision in the moment."

A short time later while walking in the park, I spotted, hanging from a tree branch, a wriggling caterpillar struggling to emerge from its cocoon. I had heard of, but had never seen, this process. I watched entranced as it slowly transformed into a brightly colored butterfly and flew away to its new life. In an "aha" instant, I realized I could no longer live inside a glass jar. Like that butterfly, I had to break out of my cocoon.

The following evening, I took my parents aside and said, "It's been two years. I've tried my best to fit in, but I'm not happy here. I must return to the United States." My parents were shocked and disappointed. They didn't understand.

"Do you really think you can live in the United States without the comfort of home, a chauffeur, a cook, a maid? Can you survive on a teacher's salary? If you leave, we're not supporting you. You're on your own."

"Fine," I answered with assurance.

With determination, confidence, and a calmness that was surprising to me I went about preparing for departure. Using my own savings, I visited friends in Europe for a month, then, en route to San Francisco, stopped in Vancouver to spend a couple of months with my nanny, Jun, by then 80 years old. She was concerned. "I'm worried. Why would you leave Hong Kong and your parents to be on your own in the U.S?" Even though there were plenty of positions for English teachers in Vancouver and I would have loved to stay with my nanny, I couldn't tolerate the dreary, chilly winter weather. The beautiful morning I arrived in San Francisco the sun warmed my back as I looked up to see the crimson hue of the majestic Golden Gate Bridge. I knew I had come home.

Fortunately, while I looked for a job, I was able to stay with my mother's sister, my Aunt Pinky, and Uncle Ben, who now lived in Oakland. I called Sister Claire Madeleine, still head of the English department at Holy Names University, and asked if I could see her. She was surprised and delighted to hear from me.

On the morning of my appointment, the skies opened up with torrential rains and howling winds. It was a tempest! Should I go or not? My intuition strongly urged me to go. So, armed with an umbrella, I headed out despite the stormy weather. When I got off the bus and began the long climb up the slope to the university, the winds and rain collapsed my umbrella and battered me mercilessly. At that moment, I longed for my parents' chauffeur to pull up and take me to the front door. I arrived at Sister Claire Madeleine's office tired and soaked.

"Why did you come in weather like this?" she asked. She hurried to get me towels and hot tea. We sat and chatted. I told her that I had returned from Hong Kong and was looking for a teaching job in order to support myself.

"Well, that's funny. I just threw away an advertisement," she said. "Notre Dame High School is looking for an English teacher." She reached down into the wastebasket beside her desk and pulled out the ad. "You should apply," she said, handing me the crumpled paper. I'll be your reference." Thanks to my intuition, I got my first job.

I was hired to teach English at a boarding school for girls in Belmont, about 30 minutes outside of San Francisco. I enjoyed the teaching. However, the position required me to live on campus in a nearby dormitory. Surrounded by students all the time, I felt isolated from everything. I had no life.

The next year, I found another job, teaching English to adults at Alemany Community College in San Francisco, but after five years, I was bored. Just then I was offered a position to teach at Bechtel, an engineering corporation in San Francisco. The company intended to expand into China and wanted to prepare its engineers by offering classes in Mandarin. It was a full-time job, with evening sessions held in the company's beautiful modern facilities and with the most updated teaching aids made available. I loved teaching there because the students were highly motivated. I made the class fun and interesting by bringing in guest speakers, planning excursions, going to restaurants, and holding speech competitions in Chinese. At the end of the first year, students rated me as "fun and effervescent."

In 1975 I would leave San Francisco to marry Peter in Honolulu. In accepting his proposal of marriage I took another road less traveled by and became the stepmother of five children, a challenge I delved into with heart and soul. Now, after 43 years of a fulfilling marriage, I am blessed with having loved five children and delighted in eleven grandchildren.

Looking back, I realize that leaving the old and welcoming the new was the best decision of my life. Freeing myself to live in the United States gave the space to spread my wings and explore life in all its possibilities—family, friends, travel, personal and spiritual growth. It was a pivotal point in setting myself free to discover my potential and to be true to myself.

Being in Charge

Harmony of the body, mind, and soul is total well-being.

— Swami Satchidananda

O*h no. It's morning.* Every time I opened my eyes it was the same. Looming before me were fatigue and listlessness. Added to these were the stress and anxiety of my application for residency in the United States. For years I didn't ever wonder about the source of my lethargy.

One overcast day I dragged myself out of bed to make a cup of tea, feeling I could not go on this way. I had to make a change. I had to do something about my health. As I glanced at the local newspaper on the kitchen table, an article about San Francisco's Integral Yoga Institute caught my eye. Something stirred. "Yoga," I whispered. "What's that?" I decided to visit the center that very day. I had absolutely no idea that my entire life and my health were about to change dramatically.

As I entered the Victorian-style house, a rich scent of wood made me feel grounded. At the top of the stairs a friendly institute member in a light peach robe came to greet me. "Hari Om," she said. "Are you new here? May I show you around?" I followed her to the library, where she pointed to the large photograph on the wall of the Integral Yoga Institute's founder, Swami Satchidananda, an Indian man in his 60s with a long white beard and a gentle smile. "This is our spiritual guru who spread and popularized hatha yoga in the Western world," she explained proudly. Being totally foreign to yoga, I asked about the guru's teachings. The essence of his teaching, she told me, is that the peace of our true nature can be reached through cultivating the harmony of body, mind, and spirit. That is accomplished through the practice of yoga, meditation, service, and peaceful living. "His favorite saying," she went on, "sums up his teaching: 'without ease there is dis-ease.'"

After this succinct overview, she led me to what is always my favorite room anywhere—the kitchen. The savory aroma of fresh whole wheat bread and curry hummus made me hungry even though they were unfamiliar to me. *How I would love to eat here!* I thought. As if reading my thoughts, she asked "Would you like to join us for lunch?"

The array of salad greens, bright beets, and golden curry were a feast for the eyes and for the taste buds. Ever since moving to the United States in 1968, I had thought I was eating a normal diet—doughnuts, pastries, fried chicken, French fries, soft drinks, canned and processed food. Now I was about to embark on an adventure with vegetarian whole food for the first time in my life.

The head of the kitchen, a young man in a white apron, spoke proudly of the organic food: "We sprout the grains and beans to make our bread and hummus. The salad greens and the herbs in the dressing are grown in our own garden. Eating whole foods means eating food that is alive—fresh and whole." His culinary lesson added depth to the lunch, after which my entire body felt nourished and revitalized. They waved good-by to me with "Om Shanti" ("Peace"). I felt light for the first time in years. My whole being felt enlivened. I drove home singing.

That visit was an "aha" moment, helping me suddenly realize the source of my fatigue. My heart was full of gratitude to the Integral Yoga Institute for showing me a path of eating for health. My life would never be the same. I now had a second chance to live a vibrant life —physically and mentally.

For the first time, I began to take responsibility for my own health. I started to learn hatha yoga and meditation, and continued to learn from Swami's teaching and from his books on inner peace and on what it means to live a life of commitment and service to others. It was a whole new world of learning how to live physically, mentally, emotionally, and spiritually—in other words, how to live a balanced life.

I try to do a variety of exercises—walking, swimming, stretching, dancing. Eating for health I originally learned from the Integral Yoga Institute. I use meat as a condiment and choose to have a variety of vegetables, preferably from the farmers' market. The journey of revitalizing my health included not only *what* I eat but understanding and directing the *reason*: eating with an intention for health.

Centering the daily fragments of my life, meditation has dramatically helped to connect to my inner self and to decrease anxiety when under stress. It has become a refuge, like going home. For a few precious minutes I am with my Self. The ease and calm from meditation has noticeably boosted my immune system.

Recently a 93-year-old Japanese woman showed me her small but exquisite garden, in which she had arranged with precise care a small waterfall, a little red bridge, a mosaic turtle, flowers, and bonsai sculpture. Seeing her enjoyment and delight gave me the idea to plant a "mind-garden" with sweet and happy memories of my loved ones and all the favorite things that make my heart sing. I often stroll through this garden to energize, revitalize, and uplift my spirit.

Ultimately, I have come to see that my health is about taking charge and doing what it takes to foster wellness of body, mind, and spirit. Now I wake up with vim and vigor, saying *Oh what a beautiful morning, Oh what a beautiful day*!

A Funny Thing Happened on the Way to Hong Kong

There are no coincidences; everything happens and everyone comes into our lives to make and help us grow.
—Oprah Winfrey

I had been living in San Francisco for several years, and by 1975, Robert Hsi and I had been dating for two years. We got along very well, sharing a love of music and finding ourselves the life of gatherings due to Robert's talented piano-playing and my joining in with his sonorous singing. Robert was charming, but I had no interest in getting married. My parents were dismayed to hear how much I loved my independence as a single woman in San Francisco.

One day I asked Robert if he knew anyone in Honolulu with whom I could make a stopover visit to break up my long annual summer trip back to Hong Kong to visit my parents. Robert thought immediately of his cousin and made a call.

"I have a family friend here who is traveling to Hong Kong," he told Peter. "Can she stay with you for a night?" For some reason, Robert didn't mention that I was his girlfriend. Peter, much older than I, was a widower. His wife had died two years earlier of cancer, leaving him with five children aged 11 to 18.

"Of course she can stay with us," Peter said, "Ask her to stay a few extra days. No one comes to Hawaii for just one night!" The arrangements were easy, but a glitch was in the offing.

That year I had been teaching Mandarin to engineers at Bechtel Corporation—work I especially loved after having taught high school students. These engineers wanted to throw me a farewell dinner to celebrate the success of the class. Taking an evening for that celebration would mean leaving on a much later flight that would bypass Honolulu. I was eager to get to Hong Kong, so I decided to accept their invitation and skip Honolulu. Then another glitch.

Almost immediately after my decision, a voice in me insisted, You *Must* Go to Honolulu. It would not let up. I felt overwhelmed. Where did it come from? Why wouldn't it leave me alone? Finally, after being plagued for several days, I gave in. "Okay," I said aloud. "I will go!" The voice stopped.

When I landed in Honolulu, Peter met me at the airport, looking stiff in a dark business suit. I was in my early 30s, carefree as a butterfly. He was a widower in his late 40s, with the responsibility of bringing up five children and running an architectural company.

We got into his car, and he turned on the radio. My favorite aria from Carmen was playing. Spontaneously, I started to hum along. This immediately put him at ease. I, too, was at ease, glad to have a friendly host. Things were so casual and relaxed that I appeared at his dining room table with a towel wrapped around my hair, which I had just washed. The children did not seem to mind. Nor did Peter. From the very beginning Peter and I found it very easy to talk. He was open-minded and flexible. Our first day together flew by. Peter was more than pleased when I suggested that we jog around Diamond Head. He was an avid jogger and had run the Honolulu marathon over 10 times.

On the second day, we had an unexpected adventure when we jumped into the waters of the Toilet Bowl in Hanauma Bay. Once in, the turmoil of rising and receding waters made it almost impossible to get out. We were greatly relieved when we were finally "flushed" out and landed on the side. As we looked back, we laughed to see part of a bikini tossing around in the water.

At some point, Peter boldly asked, "Are you and Robert serious?"

"No," I replied firmly. "I've explained to Robert that I'm not interested in getting married." My response must have given Peter confidence. That evening he took me to dinner at the Moana Hotel (now the Moana Surf Rider Hotel) in Waikiki for a dinner show. The room was crowded and noisy. We sat across from each other at a small table, watching Tahitian dancers, and listening to the pounding drums. Suddenly Peter shouted something at me. The drumming was so loud that I could barely hear him.

"What did you say?" I shouted back. There was a strange look on his face. He leaned in closer and shouted again. This time I heard every word.

"Will you marry me?" My heart pounded like the drums. To my shock and surprise, I shouted,

"Yes!" Good heavens! What was going on? Had I actually said yes? It was so unlike me! Why would I marry a man with five children after knowing him for only two days? This was happening unexpectedly and too fast. To slow things down, I invited him to come to Hong Kong to meet my parents. It was important to get their approval.

When I told my parents that I had agreed to marry a man with five children, they were curious and anxious to meet him. When Peter showed up in Hong Kong a few weeks later, my mother took him aside and had a good talk with him, even though she spoke Cantonese and he spoke Mandarin (two different dialects). He completely won her over. I was astonished at the change in my mother.

"I approve the marriage," she announced,

"But he has five children!" I protested.

"They're all going to grow up," she said reassuringly. She was relieved that I was willing to get married. Further reassurance came when Lin Yun, a renowned aura-reading specialist, who happened to be in Hong Kong, joined us on a family dinner cruise one night. In the dim evening light and without knowing anything about Peter, he declared to Peter and me, "You two will be married in half a year, and you will be together a long time." The ultimate reassurance came from my own intuition. I saw that Peter was a man of integrity, flexibility, creativity, and trustworthiness. I knew I could count on him.

At the end of summer, I went back to San Francisco, quit my job at Bechtel, packed my things, and moved from a city I loved to Honolulu. Peter and I were married on December 28,1975, six months after Lin Yun's prediction.

A week after our wedding, I had a striking dream. A phantom-like woman approached me, cradling an infant in her arms. Without uttering a single word, she tenderly handed me the baby. She was at peace. Then she turned to walk away and, without looking back, faded into thin air. When I woke up, I sensed that the apparition was Peter's deceased wife, Priscilla. A light came on. So it was *her* voice that had pressed me to come to Honolulu! She had somehow found me to take care of her children and her husband.

There were times I felt quite overwhelmed with the challenge of becoming a stepmother. I knew I could not replace the mother of the five children, aged 11 to 18. How could I fill the void in their lives, tend to their emotional needs, help them to grieve their loss? It seemed impossible. Hearing the song "Climb Every Mountain" from the *Sound of Music* gave me the answer to my prayer and inspired me to the realization of what I could do: love them with all the love I could give every day of my life for as long as I live. Being a stepmother of five helped me to grow in understanding and love—which has now been extended to 11 grandchildren.

The ultimate reward was to see the children mature into compassionate and professional men and women of integrity and to see their commitment in bringing up their own children. Being a stepmother has been daunting, but it has given such a sense of fulfillment and meaning to my life. Often I was sustained by the trust with which Priscilla had turned them over to me in the dream that revealed my destiny to marry Peter.

Family reunion at Colorado Springs 2018:
Peter and Rosanna Hsi with children
Marlene, Mark, and Paul

Inside Out

Attitude is a little thing that makes a big difference.

—Winston Churchill

When, after a whirlwind romance, I moved from San Francisco to Honolulu to marry Peter in 1975, I could not have realized I would soon be embarking on an inner journey of self-awareness. Shortly into our marriage when I sensed that Peter had a bad temper, I believed I could change him. Don't they say that love can move mountains? What a rude awakening was coming. Every time we argued, we locked horns like two bucks and fought to the bitter end, each of us fiercely determined to be right. Peter would storm out of the house, slamming the door behind him and squealing the tires as he drove away. Then I would punish him by giving him the silent treatment for days. The discord in our relationship started to disturb my sleep. I wanted to do something, but I felt helpless.

Serendipitously I came across a quote from a modern spiritual text, *A Course in Miracles*: "Would you rather be right or happy?" A light came on. It's my choice? I can choose to be happy? I don't have to be right? Choosing to withdraw from a combative attitude could open up new possibilities—to go beyond a power struggle, to choose a happy marriage. With the realization that I was responsible for my choice, I began to notice my part in our ongoing conflicts. It was difficult to look within myself and recognize that I participated in the setup that caused the upset!

An opportunity to apply this insight soon presented itself when Peter and I disagreed over the color of the granite we wanted for the kitchen. I caught myself falling into the old habit of taking on a fighting stance. He wanted black granite. I wanted white. I knew my choice was a better match. But I paused and asked if I would rather be right or happy. I took a deep breath, then softened my attitude and asked if we could compromise. Surprised to see the change, Peter agreed. Now *I* was surprised. We settled for taupe.

A new space opened up for us, a place we could enter together. In later reflection, I see it as the field that the 13th-century Sufi mystic Rumi spoke of when he said, "Out beyond right and wrong, there is a field. I'll meet you there." To me, making our way to that field meant looking for change within. It was the beginning of cultivating a greater awareness of my inner world—my thoughts, feelings, motives, attitudes. With that growing awareness, I could make a conscious choice about the direction of our marriage. As I improved my attitude, manner, and tone of voice, I could see and feel an instant ease from within that radiated out into our relationship.

The "aha" moment that came in the midst of wanting to change my husband was that change and solutions come from the inside—of myself. It was incredibly liberating to realize that my life—its quality, direction, and meaning—depended largely on my intention and the choices I made. My life is actually lived from the inside out; with my thoughts I create my reality from within. Perhaps that's what our precocious seven-year-old grandson, Matthew, meant when he said to his mother one day, "You cannot change me unless I want to. I have to work on my own self."

A few years later, in 1985, Peter survived a terrible hotel fire in Manila by using bed sheets to climb down eight stories. That close call with death made both of us want to make the most of life. To that end, we sought help from a spiritual mentor for personal and spiritual growth. Under her guidance, Peter worked at finding the source of his temper and learning to channel it positively, and I worked on being mindful of my thoughts, words, and actions. "Marriage is a temporal and spiritual journey," our counselor told us. "It offers us the opportunity for self-betterment by letting go of our habitual destructive tendencies and, above all, for loving another person more than ourselves." As we grew into harmony in the space beyond right and wrong, we also found Kahlil Gibran's "space in [our] togetherness/ And [that] the winds of heavens dance between [us]."

Peter and I continued to encourage and support each other's personal fulfillment. Over the years, Peter expanded in many ways. In addition to being an architect and engineer, he became an inventor, an entrepreneur, a ceramic artist, and even came to enjoy writing. I followed my love of French, writing, swimming, ballroom dancing, and choral singing. We are often together but also give each other the space to explore personal interests. Peter went so far in his support that he accompanied me to ballroom dancing, though dancing was not his forte. On one occasion, I was astonished to feel him dancing cheek-to-cheek. What's this? I wondered. Then I heard it: a soft snore. Peter had fallen asleep on my cheek!

Over the years I have absorbed from Peter some of his generosity of mind and heart, his deep sense of integrity, and his "can-do" attitude. Marriage, I have come to see, is much more than two people spending a life together. It is a temporal but also a spiritual journey. When I recognized and honored my spouse's spiritual and personal journey, I found I was indeed married to my soul mate. Yes, love *can* move mountains. The biggest mountain that was moved was the inner change in myself.

Three Mentors, Three Awakenings

In everybody's life, at some time, our inner fire goes out. It is then burst into flame by an encounter with another human being. We should all be thankful for those people who rekindle the inner fire.

—Albert Schweitzer

Something was gnawing at me. Something I needed to talk about. I knocked on the office door of Sister Claire Madeleine, the head of Holy Names University's English department. She was personable, and I felt very comfortable approaching her. She had taken a special interest in me, a foreign student from Hong Kong majoring in English. After inviting me in, she indicated a chair.

"How are your classes going?" she asked, as I sat down.

"I didn't realize how much writing was involved in being an English major. I'm struggling with my writing." She studied me for a few moments and then posed a perceptive question.

"Are you trying to write like someone else?" I didn't have to think about my answer.

"Oh yes," I blurted out. "I'm emulating Ernest Hemingway. I love his focused descriptions, and I'm trying so hard to write like him." Sister Madeleine leaned back in her chair.

"Hemingway? Hmm. Well, great as he may be, you don't need to imitate him. In fact, you don't need to imitate anyone at all. Write in your *own* style. Just write from your heart." Her words were disconcerting. I admired Hemingway. Shouldn't I try to write like him?

"Is it really that simple? Just write from my heart?" She nodded, smiling.

"Yes, it's that simple. If you write from the heart, you will have no problem at all."

That conversation was an awakening. For the rest of my time at Holy Names, remembering her words made it easier to write papers. Sister Madeleine's advice not only helped me through my college studies, but challenged and enabled me to finally express myself—my feelings and thoughts—from deep within—a practice that I had never been exposed to in Hong Kong. It was awkward at first. I discovered that writing from the heart meant giving attention to *what was in the heart*, reflecting honestly on what I found, allowing insight to surface, trusting myself, and believing in the value of what I had to say, even at the expense of being vulnerable.

Her words would affect my teaching as well, spurring me to find ways to get students to write from their hearts. For example, as a student teacher in a private secondary school in England, I had an English class of high school girls who hated writing. I gave them an assignment to become pen pals with a young girl who lived in Hong Kong on a traditional fishing junk. I pretended to be that young girl myself, telling them, through letters, all about my life, and asking them to write back to me and share their stories as well. The students were thrilled with this assignment. They loved that someone was interested in them, and they were excited to tell all about their very different lives in Durham, England. Most astonishing was the fact that they expressed their feelings—despite another English teacher's warning that "We English do not express our emotions." Their enthusiastic response was a testament to the effectiveness of writing from the heart.

Thanks to Sister Madeleine's words of wisdom, my love of writing continues to this day, with journaling and sometimes publishing as a freelance writer. In the 1980s, I especially enjoyed working for the *Integral Yoga* magazine on two articles about Swami Satchidananda, the Indian yogi who founded the Integral Yoga Institute and who stayed with my husband and me when he visited Honolulu.

I had been practicing yoga and loving it ever since I had discovered hatha yoga through the Integral Yoga Institute in San Francisco. Although Swami Satchidananda was the founder, I had never met him. In 1978 I learned that a silent yoga retreat would be held in Maui. Peter and I registered for the four-day event attended by about 100 people.

During the Maui retreat, we spent our days meditating, practicing yoga postures, doing volunteer service, and listening to Swami speak for many enjoyable hours. He spoke to us about respecting every faith, the value of service, and realizing the peace and purity of our true nature. His essential interfaith message, the foundation of the Integral Yoga Institute, was simple and profound: *Truth is one; paths are many.* Just as Sister Madeleine's words had awakened something in me, so did Swami's. I felt a sense of awe to be in his presence. Like everyone there, I wanted to get to know him more, but that wasn't possible because it was a silent retreat.

Two years later, Peter and I received a phone call from someone who had attended the Maui Retreat. Swami was coming to Oahu to give a talk and needed a host. Would Peter and I be willing? I was initially hesitant because I didn't know what was involved in hosting an important man like Swami. But Peter gave an enthusiastic yes, so I agreed.

Swami, a tall, dignified, and stately man with a long salt and pepper beard, arrived at our home dressed in flowing saffron robes. He was accompanied by a female secretary, another swami, to take

Swami Satchidananda
(Photo courtesy of *Integral Yoga* magazine)

care of all his travel plans. I had been tense before his arrival, but he quickly put us at ease with his relaxed and down-to-earth manner. From the time he arrived, we noticed that a tranquility and peacefulness descended on our house in a way that we had never experienced before.

During his stay we discovered his wonderful sense of humor and love of puns. One morning I was in the kitchen, assuming he was resting in his bedroom. When I looked up, I was startled to see him at my side.

"Swami, I didn't know you were there!"

"That's because I take myself lightly," he grinned. He would make puns about the soul and the sole of a shoe, about bliss and blisters. "Being enlightened," he said, "is about being light!"

He loved to look at gadgets with Peter. The two would go off to the Japanese department store Shirokiya in the Ala Moana shopping center, where they explored the latest technology, trying to figure out how things worked—like two enthusiastic young boys, bubbling with imagination and creativity, excited by the latest inventions.

Swami passed away in 2002 in India at the age of 87, leaving to the world an impactful legacy of hatha yoga and his teaching. His name, Satchidananda, in Sanskrit means existence, knowledge, bliss. Those qualities were forcefully alive in Joseph Campbell, my next mentor.

I didn't know anything about Joseph Campbell until Peter and I attended his seminar in Honolulu. I had no idea that he was the renowned author of over 20 books on mythology and that he had originated the phrase "Follow your bliss." During the workshop, I knew I was in the presence of a scholar—a man who had in-depth knowledge of Eastern and Western culture and who was imbued with, and lived, the wisdom of mythology. He was a handsome man in his 70s with a beautiful smile. An inner fulfillment seemed to shine through him and light up the room. When his wife, Jean Erdman, returned to Honolulu, Peter and I invited them to our home for dinner. We learned that they lived on the Gold Coast in Waikiki and that Jean was a dancer in the Martha Graham Dance Company.

Over the course of our friendship, he told us how much he loved the natural beauty of Hawaii, especially the ocean, which had become his muse for his daily writing. He radiated a deep contentment, and I wanted to know more about this. One evening after dinner, I asked, "Joe, you are so often quoted saying 'Follow your bliss.' What do you mean by that? Am I following my bliss when I just go shopping?" I was astonished that he treated my question, with so much respect and reverence, though it sounded silly."

"On one level, following your bliss can mean just following your fancy," he said, "like going shopping. But another level of following our bliss is to find and follow our life's purpose, to move toward fulfillment. The privilege of a lifetime is to be who we really are." The joy that Joseph Campbell exuded came from his integration of living his truth, carrying out his purpose, following his bliss, and becoming who he really was.

These three mentors—Sister Claire Madeleine, Swami Satchidananda, and Joseph Campbell—significantly rekindled my inner fire by awakening in me the courage to respect my own voice, to live from within, and to fulfill my purpose in life. Their gifts have contributed to, and continue to guide, my life.

Light and Love

It is better to light a candle than to curse the darkness.

—Chinese proverb (but also variously attributed)

The social consciousness fostered by the Maryknoll Convent School in Hong Kong has issued in my commitment to volunteer work as an important way to give back to the community. This began with the Catholic Legion of Mary; continued later with the Red Cross in San Francisco, where I helped the blind with everything from writing letters to escorting them to concerts; and has flourished with music therapy in Honolulu.

Music, especially singing, has always been part of my life, so I was intrigued to read in the newspaper about Professor Arthur Harvey, a music educator from the University of Hawaii, who had created a music therapy program for chronically ill patients in the hospital. I had witnessed the healing power of music in my own life. What stood out in the article was that he ended each music session with the song "You are My Sunshine." I called with an offer to help.

Dr. Harvey sang with a rich tenor voice, was a gifted pianist, and had talented musicians to accompany him. I became the logistics person, doing what I do best—engaging the patients and getting them to participate.

Nearly all of the patients were elderly and were in long-term care or would never leave the hospital. Most were in wheelchairs, and some in wheel beds. I naturally gravitated to the patients, encouraging them

*Dr. Harvey and I at Leahi Hospital
with a patient*
(Photo courtesy of *Integral Yoga* magazine)

to sing along. Dr. Harvey would play and sing songs from all over the world, depending on the ethnic backgrounds of the patients on any given day. Though there were songs from several countries, the favorites were always Hawaiian, which all of them had learned in childhood.

I saw how the music enlivened them. An Asian woman rose out of her wheelchair to dance. I lent her my shoulder to help with balance. An elderly twisted and hunched man started singing along with "Somewhere over the Rainbow." An Irish woman grasped the microphone to give a solo rendition of "When Irish Eyes Are Smiling," her own eyes glistening with memory. The patients entered the room like withered leaves, heads drooping, eyes half closed, bodies stiff and, by the end when we sang "You Are My Sunshine," they were opened up to us—happy, awake, and thankful—enlivened witnesses to the universal healing power of music.

Eventually, however, Dr. Harvey would retire to Florida, and gradually his musicians would also leave. I remember the day we announced to the patients that the music therapy program would be discontinued. I saw tears in their eyes. After feeling a void for months, I decided to approach the hospital to see if I could take over the program. They agreed. Now three enthusiastic musician-singers work with me—ukulele, bass, and guitar players—and I still do what I do best: work among the patients.

I have added physical exercises to the singing and music so the patients get a fuller benefit. In addition, I started a "Leahi Band" (named after the hospital) in which patients play a variety of percussion instruments. We open each session singing "Getting to Know You," during which I give each of them the "high five." Songs are interspersed with calling out three times "Hip, Hip Hooray!" We end with "You Are My Sunshine" and a final "Hip, Hip Hooray!" Each session has a musical theme—Japanese, Korean, Hawaiian, calypso, or even country western. We dance with our hands, using the hula gestures. To activate alertness and hand agility, we throw a small stuffed animal to one another. During the game, their quick response always surprises me.

Recently, I noticed teary eyes in Etta, an elderly woman, who worked her way over to me.

"Why are you crying?" I asked.

"It's so good of all of you to come here every week and make us happy," she whispered gratefully. If music brings healing and lightness into lives of the patients, it also brings me indescribable joy and gratification.

In an ever-evolving awareness of the needs of others, I've also discovered that sometimes the light that people need is literally the light of day. That realization stirred in me as I watched the CNN Heroes of the Year program. Dr. Laura Stachel, an obstetrician, was nominated as one of the top ten Heroes for 2013. She had visited Nigeria and Uganda to investigate the high infant mortality rates. The CNN program showed her standing with a Nigerian midwife in a very dark hut, a makeshift clinic with absolutely no electricity at night. The midwife showed Dr. Stachel how she would have to deliver a baby at night, using the tiny undependable light of her cell phone or, even worse, a kerosene lamp.

That dire situation led Dr. Stachel to encourage her husband, a solar energy expert in California, to invent a portable, solar suitcase. The suitcase used sunlight to charge during the day, and then at night it could provide light to the clinic. I became very excited watching Dr. Stachel's story because her project, We Care Solar, resonated with my lifelong motto, "It's better to light a candle than to curse the darkness." How wonderful to have an invention like this that could literally give entire communities light and life! I knew I had to get involved but had absolutely no idea how to contact Dr. Stachel.

Strangely enough, a few days later, a phone call from Dr. Bradley Wong, a friend whose nonprofit work I also support, called to tell me about a woman named Laura Stachel who was offering to give him solar suitcases for his medical mission in Nepal. I could hardly believe what I was hearing! It was true, then, that when one sets a powerful intention, the Universe rises in support. With the information he gave, I immediately contacted Dr. Stachel. My first project with her in 2014 was Power Up Gambia. I've been committed to We Care Solar ever since, supporting solar suitcase projects in Nigeria, Ethiopia, Tanzania, and Zimbabwe. The project to light up childbirth has had far-reaching benefits in many other countries by providing sustainable energy for around-the-clock medical light and power for fetal monitoring devices. Saving a mother saves a child, which in turn saves a fam-

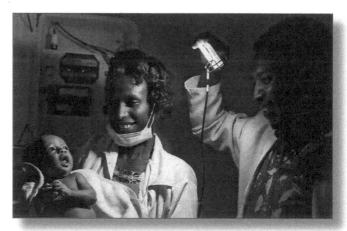

We Care Solar provides light (powered by suitcase on the wall) for nighttime births.
(Photo courtesy of We Care Solar)

ily and stabilizes a community. As Melinda Gates says in her recent book, "when you lift up women, you lift up humanity."

A Whole New World

I am part of all that I have met;
Yet all experience is an arch wherethrough
Gleams that untravelled world, whose margin fades
For ever and for ever when I move.

—Alfred Lord Tennyson

Mesmerized, I thumbed through the deck of travel cards filled with photographs of Pan American Airlines's travel destinations. My mother's friend, who worked for Pan Am, had come to visit her in Hong Kong and, as a gift, had given these tantalizing vignettes of a whole new world to this 14-year-old teenager, who had never traveled outside of the small island of Hong Kong: the Eiffel Tower, the Coliseum, the Bavarian Neuschwanstein Castle, the Pyramids, the Taj Mahal. The seed of a zest for travel was planted; I *must* see the world!

A Chinese saying observes that *it is better to travel a thousand miles than to read a thousand books*. From my decades of traveling, I would add that the fullness of travel comes from seeing the magnificence of the world, meeting new people, experiencing everything with all the senses, and taking those experiences in with the whole person—body, mind, and spirit.

One of the most breathtaking natural beauties I've ever seen was the Annapurna Mountain Range of the Himalayas. Flying from Dhaka in Bangladesh, the plane dipped its wing as we approached Katmandu, the capital of Nepal. "It's a clear, sunny morning," the pilot announced. "On your left is the Annapurna Range. Mount Everest is one of the most challenging and treacherous mountain-climbing sites in the world." I gazed out, enthralled with the icy chiseled range, showcasing the majestic Mount Everest from afar, a wind-carved jagged peak of dazzling ice, a monument to nature in all its glory. That stunning view of the Annapurna Range has never left me.

Besides the beauties of nature, travel also connects one to architectural beauty, such as is found in Barcelona's towering cathedral, the iconic Sagrada Familia, designed by the late 19th-century architect Antoni Gaudi. The heavy baroque exterior of this architectural masterpiece contrasts sharply with the airiness of the interior. Inside, innumerable columns, with carvings of leaves at the top, give the feeling of a great forest stretching up to a central dome. Natural light pours down into the cathedral and, through the stained glass windows, spreads a rich, luminous glow through the whole space. It is a touch of the sublime.

Peter and I at the Taj Mahal

Far away from Europe, I fulfilled a dream to see one of the Seven Wonders of the World, the Taj Mahal, built by Shah Jahan, as a memorial to his favorite wife, Mumtaz Mahal. The Mughal architecture of an ivory marble central dome and four corner minarets is magnificent on its own, but equally striking are the color shifts of the marble—dazzling white at midday, pearl pink at dusk, a cold splendor in the moonlight.

Discovering new cuisines is another of my favorite travel experiences. I love the adventure of exploring scents and tastes—multicolored tomatoes, and lavender products of all kinds from the farmers' market in France; organic basil, oregano, and olive oil of Italian country fairs; the burned orange of spices like turmeric, curry, and cinnamon in the Istanbul bazaars. In India, I savored the infinite creativity of curries and vegetarian dishes. In Japan, the exquisite presentation of the *kaiseki* (various courses of the chef's creation) is itself a work of art. The three essentials of Chinese fine dining are sight, smell, and taste, which make it one of the world's greatest cuisines. Hong Kong is the best place for experiencing the foods of the world, but nowhere else on the globe can surpass it in providing the inexhaustible variety of Chinese cooking from the north to the south of China. When returning to Hong Kong to visit my family, sharing good food is always a priority.

The sound of music can enhance a trip and makes it memorable. I have listened to the Berlin Philharmonic in Germany, to "The Marriage of Figaro" in Vienna, to "Ernani" at La Scala in Italy, and to "The Phantom of the Opera" in London. Each level of the Music House in Vienna showcases a particular aspect of music, such as sounds, composers, instruments. In one area, I "virtually conducted" Strauss's "The Blue Danube." Because the music itself is actually pre-recorded, it did not seem important to work hard at conducting with precision, but when I began to lag in the beat, so did the music. If I dropped my arms, the music ceased!

Traveling also spurred me in a totally unexpected direction. Many years ago, while visiting a close friend in Paris, I found myself extremely frustrated in not being able to speak French to my friend's mother, Madame Madeleine. I vowed to learn French to communicate with her. Learning the language was more challenging than I ever expected it to be, but I persisted. I wanted to keep my promise. When I returned to Paris a few years later, I proudly told Madame in my new language, "I learned French just for you." She was delighted! We talked almost non-stop for the whole visit, and we've been good friends ever since.

Sometimes the journey has been an inner one of going deeper into myself. In India, I was pushed to my limit in being exposed to a culture of extreme wealth and poverty. I had been awed by the vision of the Taj Mahal, but my senses were overwhelmed elsewhere with the human suffering in the midst of smells and sights of rats, flies, urine, cows; it was common to see children with no limbs, begging for attention in the middle of traffic, or tourists who literally passed out because of the filth. It was almost impossible to wrap my mind around it. Mother Teresa transformed poverty into love, saying "When I see those beggars, I see God, and I pray for them. I send them loving kindness." It was especially in India that the disparities of human life struck me. Remembering her words enabled me to see beyond the depressive surroundings.

I'll never forget the elderly Japanese woman I met in Katmandu when I was in my 30s, traveling alone because Peter was working on a hotel project in Dhaka, Bangladesh. We were in a crowded hotel dining room, filled with dozens of men and their gear for trekking the Himalayas with Sherpas. Curious, and fascinated by seeing just one woman—a senior among the young trekkers—I asked if I could join her. She gave a welcoming smile, and we started to talk.

"What brought you here?" I asked.

"I hope to trek to the base camp of the Himalayas accompanied by a Sherpa," she told me enthusiastically. I could hardly believe it. That feat was physically daunting for someone decades younger.

"Why are you doing this?" I asked. Her eyes burned with determination.

"The passion for challenge is what drives me," she said. She was an example of growing old boldly. Her spirit has stayed with me and has inspired me to live boldly in the face of challenge.

A challenge that I never saw coming confronted me when I was traveling alone and awoke in New Delhi, India, on October 31, 1984, to learn that Prime Minister Indira Gandhi had been assassinated by her Sikh bodyguards. Ferocious mobs poured into the streets, seeking revenge on the Sikhs. Sikh temples and taxis were burned, and drivers went into hiding. With the breakdown of public transportation, there was no way to get to the airport. How would I safely make the flight to Hong Kong? After being stranded for a day, it occurred to me that the Thai Airline crew, which was staying in the same hotel, must have some way to the airport. I tracked down the flight purser, persuaded him to take me with the crew in the airline bus, and then doggedly followed him around to make sure he would not forget me. Tensions were high in that bus as we made our way through the night curfew and held our collective breath through many checkpoints. I wept with relief when we made it to safety. The unexpected adventure in New Delhi revealed something I hadn't known about myself—an inner resourcefulness and courage in the face of crisis.

Travels have taken me across the globe to almost every continent. I have seen a range of differences—wealth, poverty, kindness, rudeness, joy, suffering, inclusiveness, and intolerance. In my world expanded and enriched by travel, I have been helped and welcomed by total strangers, have been able to communicate heart-to-heart without a shared language, and have found common experiences. Once in Katmandu, I was dismayed to learn that the donkey hired to take me through the village was to be led by a small boy who was obviously very tired. After a few minutes, I had the idea to invite him to get on the donkey, and I would do the leading. He was unwilling at first, but I helped him up, and he sat there beaming as we started our journey downhill. Villagers came out of their homes to stare in disbelief and clap with delight. Soon all of us were laughing at the role-reversal. It was a moment of togetherness although we did not share a language or culture.

There is nothing more mind- and heart-opening than travel. In the words of Mark Twain, it is "fatal to prejudice, bigotry, and narrow-mindedness." Through travel, I have gained a deepened awareness of the innate goodness and oneness of humanity. We are one, says the Dalai Lama, because our basic nature is the same. That oneness makes us interconnected and therefore interdependent. We all pray for the same things: peace, a loving family, happiness, well-being. We all want to be appreciated, respected, and loved. Ultimately, we are one human family.

Dreams Are within Reach

Let yourself be silently drawn
By the strange pull
Of what you really love, and
It will not lead you astray.

—Rumi

Never give in—never, never, never, never, in nothing great or small, large or petty, never give in except to convictions of honor and good sense. Never yield to force; never yield to the apparently over-whelming might of the enemy. Winston Churchill's indomitable spirit surges through the words he spoke to schoolboys at his alma mater in 1941. That spirit gave the British people courage to hold out for victory in World War II, led Churchill to his own victory over a stroke that had threatened to leave him an invalid with a speech impediment, and even now inspires me to overcome great odds to fulfill my dreams.

When I learned how Winston Churchill's rhetoric swayed history against the Nazis, I became aware of the power of words and longed to be able to express myself without fear, especially in public. It is said that public speaking is feared more than death. To me, it seemed worse. In dying, I thought, one could close one's eyes and quietly go away. But why would I want to go through the trauma of a roomful of eyes staring at me as I desperately fumbled around trying to say something?

The longing to speak effectively, though shunted aside as I pursued other interests, broke into my consciousness every so often, when I would again push it away. But one day in 1988 it reared its head just as I came across information on Toastmasters. It seemed to say, "Look, here's your chance. Don't push me off any more. Maybe you can actually do this." With some trepidation, I called to ask about attending a meeting, and then tried for days to find an excuse not to go. That first early morning meeting was the beginning of four years of vigorous training which included such things as practicing extemporaneous and carefully prepared speeches, crafting effective openings and endings, incorporating humor and storytelling—all this while striving to maintain confidence. The obstacles in the beginning were clammy hands, pounding heart, a blank mind, and desperation. In spite of all that, I visualized myself as a poised, competent speaker and moved step-by-step through the program. Toward the end of my training, I started to enter competitions—and win. Today I am delighted that my fear of public speaking has been transformed into a voice freed to speak my mind. My proudest moment came in speaking at a Castle Hospital workshop, where I advocated for a more sensitive and compassionate approach to health care. Toastmasters has given me the skill and the confidence to articulate my values and vision and, above all, to stand up for myself and others.

Another dream began to grow when, at the age of 12, I listened every week to Edith Piaf over Radio Hong Kong. Her distinctive expressive voice exuded the mysterious charm of La Seine in Paris, planting the seed of a Francophile in me. In 1975 the interest in French culture was reignited when my friend Louie Madeleine invited me to visit his parents in Bassou outside of Paris. They were gracious hosts, but the only way I could tell them of my gratitude or ask questions or listen to their stories was through Louie. Frustrated by not being able to communicate with them and, above all, not being able to express my gratitude for their hospitality, I promised Madame Madeleine I would learn French for her. Little did I know what would be involved.

It was the beginning of a long and arduous journey, during which I would sometimes despair of learning the subtleties of French pronunciation or mastering the complex grammar. The latter was especially foreign to me because my native dialect, Cantonese, is primarily tonal.

Furthermore, I did not have the advantage of having heard French in those early years when the brain can most easily absorb language. I was starting much later. For years I continued to struggle week after week with a private tutor. Sometimes the words of the Italian businessman, Guido Monzino urged me on: "Step by step, the goal will be attained."

To improve fluency, I spent nearly two weeks with Françoise and Bernard Ribot, good friends in Toulouse. With that immersive experience came a breakthrough in confidence, but by the time I left, my brain was ready to go on strike from the intense focus. The pitfalls of learning French never stopped. I've gone through feeling embarrassed and humiliated for my mistakes to finally being able to laugh with others at myself. I had to learn when to use the small words that made a difference between pointing out a lawyer (*Il est avocat*) or an avocado (*C'est un avocat*). Once, trying to acknowledge to a French-speaking friend that I was petite, I self-assuredly told her that I was *mignonne* ("cute").

I kept my promise to Madame Madeleine. What a reward it was to finally be able to communicate with her, to share nonstop for hours, which allowed us to get to know each other! The language enriched my understanding and appreciation of the historical wealth and depth of French culture and its contribution to humanity.

My best kept secret: a blank book on my shelf. I had placed it there sometime in my teens, feeling deep down that someday I would write a book. That dream was an inner glow that, year after year, was neither extinguished nor fanned into full flame. Decades later Peter would fulfill two of his dreams when I initiated the 2016 production of an album of professional photographs of the house he had designed and encouraged him to write his memoir, *Along the Way* (2017).

The happiness and satisfaction I felt for him was marred by the pestering of an inner voice. "What about your abandoned dream—*your* book? What are you waiting for?" I answered with an echo of the question and an elaborate answer. "What am I waiting for? Yes, of course I am waiting for perfection—when everything is right. The right time, when there are no distractions; the right condition, when there are no other obligations; the right life, when peace and calm prevail." I had been waiting...waiting...waiting...for over five decades. That time and condition and life had never come.

I heard myself asking another question: "Are you setting yourself up for failure? Are you sabotaging your dream by waiting for a situation that does not exist?" Then it struck me that, as Eckhart Tolle says, every possibility is in the Now. Suddenly I saw that the right time was NOW; that is as good as it gets. I blew the dust off the blank book I had left on the shelf for decades and wrote "It's never too late."

My choice to write a book of introspection has been both challenging and satisfying. At times I have wondered if I was being too personal or if some stories were disrespectful of my parents. Even as I saw that my intention was in the right place and gave myself permission to continue, a negative voice questioned the reason and value for writing. Why are you doing this? Isn't it a waste of time? Who cares? In spite of such bombardment, I have pressed on in the commitment to fulfill a long-held dream. Doing so has shown me the tapestry of my life, and sharing my story has been a delight.

As I write this I find another dream emerging—to help in supplying clean water to Lesotho in South Africa and to Brazil. The project is spearheaded by a Holy Names sister who is engaged with this work. My support will enable her to buy filters and other equipment, set up training programs for the local women in how to maintain the filters, and eventually to expand the program. Because clean water is so vital to life, I feel deeply drawn by this dream. It is not yet fulfilled, but I believe it is within reach and that, as Rumi says, its pull will not lead me astray.

The Source, My Parents

Appreciate the origin of the spring that quenches our thirst.

—A Chinese proverb

Mr. S. L. Ho (left) and Mrs. S. Y. Ho

My Mother

How I loved to watch my mother apply her make-up! As a 12-year-old, I sat next to her well-lit mirrored dresser, in rapt awe, as she applied the last touch to her face. The shimmer that she dabbed on her cheeks and in the corner of her eyes lit up her whole face. Her eyes gleamed, and her porcelain skin was a rose-petal blush. No wonder she was considered to be the belle of the community.

Slowly she unlocked the drawer, lifted out the dazzling diamond necklace, and beckoned the maid to help her. Just then the dinner bell summoned me. Reluctantly, I left to go down to the dining room. But when I caught the whiff of Chanel No. 5 during dinner, I darted out to gaze at my mother in her floor-length ivory lace cheongsam (traditional Chinese dress) descending the stairway, my father at her side, beaming with pride. "Mom, you look *so* beautiful, like a queen!" I exclaimed. With great effort I restrained myself from running to hug her; in our family we don't show affection that way.

All too soon, my mom's leisurely life was to be disrupted. When my father realized that providing produce for the military had no future, he hoped to give the family a better life financially by venturing into real estate development, a new field in Hong Kong in the 1950s and 1960s. It was a huge risk for a man with children, since he had no experience in a field where a single wrong decision could mean financial disaster. The worry and stress soon took a heavy toll on him physically, mentally, and emotionally. Exacerbation of pain from a curvature of the spine was forcing him to sleep in a plaster cast bed. This most uncomfortable bed led to chronic insomnia. The anxiety and depression combined made him unable to work. He was up all night, stayed in his room all day, and spoke to no one. During the day, we had to maintain quiet "so Dad can sleep." The whole house was shrouded in somberness.

My mother realized that she would have to step in if the business was to survive. Driven by her life motto, "Where there is a will, there is a way," she stepped out of her comfort zone and forged her way into the all-male world of real estate development. Although she had barely finished high school—she had been bored with school, hated it, and had often played truant—she learned the trade quickly. Quietly and self-assuredly, she surprised everyone with her insight, and vision. She was a trailblazer for women in the business world. Transformed into the dragon lady of her time, she met every challenge head-on: making successful business decisions, spearheading condominium projects, negotiating with contractors and designers, and managing construction sites, all the while dealing with my father's illness—which lasted for more than a decade.

In 1964, my mother confessed something to me that I will never forget. My parents had arrived in Oakland, California, from Hong Kong, and we were gathered at the home of my Uncle Ben and Aunt Pinky, my mother's sister, for a celebration of my graduation from Holy Names University. The apartment was crowded with my siblings as well as my uncle's mother and his five grown siblings. During the short time my parents visited me in California, my mother had the rare opportunity to see how women in the U.S. related to their children. My Uncle Ben's mother, who had come to this country from China, had raised five children on her own while working long hours as a cook in her own restaurant. Despite the innumerable hardships of a Chinese immigrant living in California, she had always found time to celebrate birthdays, to have family picnics, and to gather her family to attend church together.

A bright burst of laughter rolled through the living room. My uncle's mother smiled broadly, surrounded by her doting children. They were teasing and sharing, showing great affection to each other and their mother. Knowing there had never been this kind of warmth in our family, I watched with great curiosity to see how taken my mother was with their interactions. She had grown up in Canton, China, and with traditional Chinese values in which the primary duty of parents was to be disciplinarians. Their job was to provide things like food, clothing, shelter, and education, while the actual rearing of children was left to the amah (servant). Showing emotion to children or expressing affection for them was not a part of Chinese culture. Further, in the Hong Kong culture influenced by the English tradition, my mother had sent most of my siblings to boarding schools in England around the age of 12, which, in effect, meant, that we did not grow up with each other. I remember crying with them as they left for England. As a result of their leaving, we did not have a sense of family togetherness.

I was the oldest of six children, but always felt isolation and loneliness. Because my sisters and brothers had been sent off to boarding school, I was the only one at home when my mother took my ailing father to Japan for medical treatment. I seem to have spent almost all my teenage years wandering around a huge mansion, sometimes accompanied by my nanny, and always by my dog Lolo. But there was no family life. When I was chosen to represent the school in the annual speech contest, I felt alone in a hall full of students, all of whose parents were with them. What I looked forward to each year was the return of my siblings for the brief summers, which brought the only occasions when we spent time as a family on my father's yacht, swimming in Clear Water Bay.

Now, at my graduation celebration, my mother motioned to me to follow her into the kitchen. When we were alone, she spoke. "I had no idea," she said, shaking her head. "I never thought I was doing anything wrong by not bringing you up myself." She paused, looked at me directly, with eyes full of sadness and regret. "I don't know any of my children," she confessed in a whisper. Her honesty shocked me. It was a precious moment of truth between us. It was also a moment of poignancy because she seemed to realize she had missed that special window of time when the bonding with children can take place.

As I grew older and matured, I started to appreciate the heavy load my mother had shouldered and how she had managed. In spite of the mental and emotional duress she had gone through with my father's long debilitating illness and the demands of the business, she did her best in her circumstances to meet the needs of her children. Nor did she forget to think of those who were less fortunate. "Whatever we reap from the community, we must give back," she told us. Her deeds were true to her word. When she learned that the Haka women in the Chinese countryside had to walk miles to give birth, a sense of compassion moved her to alleviate that hardship by building a hospital in Hing Ning. To honor her legacy of philanthropy after her death, my sister Jean initiated a charitable foundation in our mother's name to finance proactive measures in the community to counteract dementia in Hong Kong.

My mother's gifts to me were to have courage, to be adaptable, to persevere in adversity, and, above all, to give back to the community. Her whole life exemplified her motto: where there is a will there is a way.

My Father

My vivid memory of being eight years old is of looking out of our living room window at five o'clock and watching the lanky silhouette of my father leave home in the dim, cold light of a wintry morning. He was going to work.

In Hong Kong, my father had started out supplying the English military with fresh produce, a tiring job that forced him to keep early and long hours. He quickly realized that that career was a dead end, and he began to envision possibilities as a real estate developer. It was the mid-1950s, and Hong Kong was a potential gold mine in that field. He decided to seize the opportunity.

My father knew nothing about real estate and had to learn everything from scratch. Because of his conscientiousness and good timing, his business succeeded from the beginning. As a result, he purchased a piece of prized property on a hill and built a stately three-story house for us with a pavilion, a badminton court, and a swing in the garden. But the unrelenting stress of the business triggered a chronic illness.

Mr. S. L. Ho (left) and Mrs. S. Y. Ho

Coming from the same social norms as my mother had, he never sought closeness with us. He was reticent and also a recluse, so we never felt we knew him. Because I was the oldest child, I sensed something was wrong when his isolation intensified. After the onset of his illness, my mother traveled with him on the ocean liner the President Wilson to receive medical treatment in

Japan. When they returned a month later, my mother whispered to me, "We must hide all sharp objects from your father." As a 15-year-old, I was frightened.

Some days later, on a beautiful summer day, I found myself standing outside my father's room. I wanted to see him. I wanted to talk to him. Timidly, I knocked on his door. No response. I knew he was inside. Again I knocked, then went in.

The room was dark. Dad was sitting on the couch, looking blankly ahead. I stood there for a moment, not sure what to do. He didn't look up. Then something welled up inside me. I walked over and sat down next to him.

"I wanted to talk to you, Dad," I began, my throat tight. "I wanted to tell you… I wanted to say…." I hesitated. His eyes still stared ahead. "I wanted to tell you that we all love you and you are important to us. You have so much to live for…." I don't remember what I said after that but I talked to him for hours. He never said a word to me. I knew he was listening. I talked about his horses—feeding them carrots at the stable. He adored his horses (many of whom were named after the produce he had supplied years earlier—names like American Carrot or Spanish Onion). He was one of the most respected racehorse owners in Hong Kong. I talked about our swimming, the ice cream cone he always bought me afterwards, and spending time on his yacht. I just kept talking….

Something profound happened that day. I had cracked his shell, and he had let me in. A bond formed between us—not discernible by external signs, but on a deep level. From that day on, things were different. I was able to show him affection by massaging his neck and shoulders to release the tightness and by engaging him in every way I could—talking with him about his horses, keeping him company when he went on his boat or went swimming.

In his 70s, my father was diagnosed with pancreatic cancer. I was with him at home and in the hospital in Hong Kong for the last few weeks of his life. Since my brother David was in Hong Kong, he came often and sat by his side.

One day, after David had left and I was with my father in his room, he turned to me and said, "I didn't realize David was such a fine man, such a caring person." His eyes were moist, and I recognized the same flicker of sadness and regret I had seen in my mother's eyes years ago in Oakland. "I didn't know David," he admitted quietly.

When my father passed away at the age of 73, it was hard to let him go, but I felt I had come to know him. I was glad that he and David had had a chance to connect. Many of the villagers and community leaders came to the funeral service to acknowledge the school he had built in China, a school now known for the quality of its students. I still share the passions my father passed on to me—the love of horses, swimming, and ballroom dancing.

From both of my parents, I learned to show affection by connecting

My siblings and I with our mother:
Front L to R: Robert Ho, our mother, Jean Ho, and Agnes Ho
Back L to R: Rose Hofmann and I

with them at whatever level was possible. But, strangely, the very things that were absent—physical closeness to, emotional intimacy with, and understanding of their children—are the very things I have learned to cultivate and treasure. Even though love is often sensed and experienced, at the same time it is important to express and communicate appreciation and affection. I can never assume that others know I love and care for them. That care must be shown and put into words and action. This is why I have always tried, in every way possible, to express to my family and friends how much they mean to me.

Paths to Harmony

As a child, I heard the very common Chinese saying "A peaceful life is a happy life" and thought, How boring! Who wants peace? I want excitement! In seeking excitement, especially as I grew older, I became overwhelmed with activities and socializing, hardly stayed home at all, and in fact went overboard in many aspects of my life. Without enough rest, without a balanced diet, and with a house cluttered from shopping sprees, I felt driven—but driven to what? To find a happy life? In Albert Einstein's view, a peaceful life, not constant outer pursuits, brings the most happiness.

The urgency of needing to regain balance led me to reconsider Buddha's Middle Path and his analogy of a stringed instrument: when the strings are too loose or too tight, he observed, the sound is not harmonious. Because the analogy so accurately pinpointed my life, it struck me deeply. That Buddhist attitude is consistent with the Chinese principle that health hinges on balance of the whole person. I therefore made a commitment to myself, as part of my spiritual practice, to look within and be aware of swinging from one extreme to the other. What I have found most useful in this attempt is visualizing an inner steering wheel that helps me to sensitively adjust my direction whenever I'm off course. My life continues to be a seesaw, an endless balancing act.

In aspiring to live a peaceful life, I discovered that I couldn't think myself into peacefulness. I had to appreciate its value and take time to savor it. That opportunity came by experiencing its total absence in 2014, when, out of nowhere, I contracted a lung infection that led to an 18-month roller coaster ride of doctors, medicine, and suffering. The first prognosis was that there would be recovery but that the infection would recur and I would again be on antibiotics. Only after a second opinion (at National Jewish Health Hospital in Denver) diagnosed acid reflux and delivered me from chaos did I fully appreciate what it meant to have peace and calm. Now I value being still and letting go of the need to grasp, get, do, or fight. I can just be—a life moment to relish. Quiet time has become an important part of my daily spiritual practice.

Oprah Winfrey, also a great source of spiritual inspiration to me, has shown a way to handle those things that threaten to disrupt peace. She has popularized the phrase "the aha moment," describing it as an instant of seeing something in a new and revealing light. I watched her on television as she helped a grieving woman to see that the death of a loved one didn't have to be only sorrowful; it could also be the chance to be grateful for, and appreciative of, the life that the deceased person had led; it could be a celebration. The grieving woman had an aha moment when she realized this.

One of my own most insightful aha moments came on the day I felt the result of my bad habit of mentally criticizing other people. During a vacation in Italy, I was with a group of American tourists, when a stranger from the group, out of nowhere, came over and publically criticized me. I was shocked. Why was she doing this? Had I done something to her? Then a light came on. I suddenly realized that what she was doing to me was what I had mentally been doing to other people all along. Until then, I had always thought that only external words and actions reaped karma. I had had no idea that thoughts also come back to us. I saw the far-reaching consequence of the principle that for every action there is an equal reaction. Having experienced firsthand the boomerang effect of getting back what I put out, it has become an important spiritual practice for me to cautiously and vigilantly plant good karma through my every thought, word, action, and intention.

Possibilities for aha moments abound. They can lead us to break— or to find a breakthrough. The breakthrough may be, for example, seeing death in the light of gratitude for life. We simply need to be open to discovering aha moments by looking for the hidden gifts and lessons in life's challenges. This is consistent with Buddhist spiritual teaching, which sees adversity as an opportunity for epiphany. Seizing the aha moment, following the Middle Path, and savoring peace, have put me on the way to living a life of harmony.

As I look back on this essay and those that have come before, I notice that I have drawn inspiration and have learned from both the East and the West— from the Buddha and Winston Churchill, from Asian wisdom and Western thinkers, from Confucianism and Christianity. The seamless back and forth movement extends to conversations with Peter, when, without thinking, we are totally at home with speaking both Chinese and English. When I took the leap to move from Hong Kong to the U.S. many years ago, it was not to turn my back on a rich tradition, but to grow beyond the East and West. From the West, I have especially appropriated the heritages of England and France and have appreciated the breath of fresh air, innovative creativity, and open spirit of the U.S. Embracing these was tempered by a secure rootedness in the culture of my birth. In merging the two cultures, I am grateful to both of them for immensely enriching my life and for the wisdom and harmony I have found in their gifts.

The yin yang symbol is my inspiration to live a balanced and harmonious life.

Reflection

*I*t is my heritage, experiences, family, and the many inspiring mentors and friends in my life that have nurtured me and contributed to who I am. Above all, it is my spiritual path that continues to uplift me and give substance and meaning to my life. For these I am blessed and deeply grateful.

May I not be a bystander
But a catalyst
For benevolence.

Where there is impasse,
Be the change;
Solution begins with me.

Where there are barriers,
Be open to the "aha,"
Seek the light for awakening.

Where there is indifference,
Be the caring;
Kindness begets kindness.

Where there is apathy,
Fuel the inner passion
That soars with wings.

Where there is want,
Let surge my bounty,
So abundance may flow.

Where there is inadequacy,
Look within.
Wisdom is there.

CPSIA information can be obtained
at www.ICGtesting.com
Printed in the USA
LVHW071927230719
625036LV00007B/10/P